KARLA BONNARD

AI ART

The Future of Creativity and How to Profit from It!

This book was professionally typeset on Reedsy.
Find out more at reedsy.com

"The only way to discover the limits of the possible is to go beyond them into the impossible."

- Arthur C. Clarke

Contents

1

Introduction

"Artificial intelligence is the new electricity." - Andrew Ng, co-founder of Coursera and former chief scientist of Baidu

Artificial intelligence (AI) is transforming every aspect of our lives, from health care to education, from entertainment to transportation. But what about art? Can AI help us create and appreciate art in new and exciting ways? Can AI enable us to express our creativity, reach a wider audience, and generate income from our art? And what are the challenges and opportunities of using AI for art in 2024 and beyond?

These are some of the questions that motivated me to write this book. As an artist and a technology lover, I have always been fascinated by the intersection of AI and art, and how they can inspire and complement each other. I have also witnessed the rapid growth and evolution of AI and art in the past few years, and how they have opened up new possibilities and platforms for artists and art lovers.

In this book, I will share with you my passion, experience, and vision for the future of AI and art. I will also introduce you to the main concepts and terms related to AI and art, such as artificial intelligence, machine learning, generative art, and creative coding. I will explain what they mean, how they work, and how they are used in art creation and appreciation.

I will also give you an overview of the book's structure and content, and how it will help you to use AI to create and sell art online in 2024. In each chapter, I will cover a different topic, technique, tool, or platform that you can use to enhance your artistic skills and projects. I will also provide you with practical examples, exercises, and tips that you can apply to your own art.

By the end of this book, you will be able to:

- Understand the basics and the state-of-the-art of AI and art
- Use AI to generate, analyze, and optimize your art
- Use creative coding to design and program your own art
- Use generative art to create unique and original art
- Use online platforms and marketplaces to showcase and sell your art
- Use social and online communities to promote and grow your art business

This book will inspire you to explore, experiment, and innovate with AI and art, and to discover your own creative potential and expression. I hope this will also help you to achieve your artistic goals and dreams, and to profit from your passion and talent.

Are you ready to join me on this journey of discovery, exploration, and innovation in the world of AI and art? If so, let's get started!

Chapter 1: The evolution and revolution of AI and art

A I and art have a long and rich history of interaction and collaboration, dating back to the mid-20th century. In this chapter, I will explore evolution and revolution of AI and art, from the early experiments and pioneers to the current trends and innovations. I will also discuss the impact and challenges of AI and art, such as the ethical, social, and legal issues, the role of human creativity and agency, and the changing nature and value of art. I will also showcase some of the most famous and influential AI artists and artworks in the world, and how they inspire and challenge the conventional notions of art and aesthetics.

The early experiments and pioneers of AI and art

The origins of AI and art can be traced back to the 1950 and 60's when computer scientists and artists began to experiment with the potential of using computers to generate, analyze, and manipulate art. Some of the early examples of AI and art include:

- **A. Michael Noll**, who created some of the first computer-generated artworks, such as **Gaussian-Quadratic**, a geometric abstraction based on a mathematical formula, and **Computer Composition with Lines**, a simulation of Mondrian's style using a random number generator.
- **Harold Cohen**, who developed **AARON**, a computer program that could autonomously produce original drawings and paintings, based on a set of rules and knowledge about art and visual perception.
- **Frieder Nake**, who applied **algorithmic art**, a form of generative art that uses algorithms to create complex and unpredictable patterns and shapes, such as **Matrix Multiplication**, a series of plots based on matrix operations.
- **Leon Harmon and Kenneth Knowlton**, who created **Studies in Perception**, a collection of images that used computer-generated symbols and dots to create portraits and landscapes, a **pixelated representation** of those types of objects.

These and other pioneers of AI and art demonstrated the possibility and diversity of using computers as creative tools and partners, and laid the foundations for the future developments and innovations in the field.

The current trends and innovations of AI and art

In the past few decades, AI and art have undergone a rapid and radical transformation, thanks to the advancements in computer hardware, software, and algorithms, as well as the emergence of new platforms and communities for art creation and distribution. Some of the current trends and innovations of AI and art include:

- **Machine learning**, a branch of AI that enables computers to learn from data and experience, and to perform tasks that are difficult or impossible to program explicitly, such as image recognition, natural language processing, and recommendation systems. Machine learning has enabled artists to create new and novel forms of art, such as **style transfer**, a technique that applies the style of one image to another, such as **The Starry Night over the Rhone**, a combination of Van Gogh's and Monet's paintings, and **neural style**, a method that generates artistic images from scratch, such as The Next Rembrandt, a portrait of a man that resembles the style of the Dutch master.

- **Generative adversarial networks (GANs)**, a type of machine learning model that consists of two competing neural networks, one that generates fake data and one that tries to distinguish between real and fake data. GANs have enabled artists to create realistic and diverse images, videos, and sounds, such as **This Person Does Not Exist**, a website that generates realistic faces of people who do not exist, **DeepFake**, a technique that swaps the faces of celebrities in videos, such as **Face-off**, a video that replaces the faces of Nicolas Cage and John Travolta in the movie Face/Off, and **Jukebox**, a system that generates music and lyrics in the style of various artists, such as **Frank Sinatra singing Toxic**, a song that mimics the voice and style of the legendary crooner.

- **Creative coding**, a form of programming that uses code as a medium of artistic expression and exploration, rather than as a tool for solving problems or performing tasks. Creative coding has enabled artists to design and program their own art, using languages and frameworks such as **Processing, p5.js**, and **openFrameworks**, and to create interactive and immersive experiences, such as **The Coding Train**, a YouTube channel that teaches creative coding through fun and engaging projects, **The Art of Code**, a TEDx talk that demonstrates the beauty and power of code as art, and **The EyeWriter**, a device that allows people with paralysis to draw with their eyes.

[handwritten annotations: New methods of medicine? Technically a Biomedical device, gives a disability a novel form of expression]

These and other trends and innovations of AI and art have expanded the scope and scale of artistic expression and experimentation, and have opened up new possibilities and platforms for artists and art lovers.

The impact and challenges of AI and art

AI and art have not only changed the way we create and appreciate art, but also the way we think and feel about art. AI and art have raised various questions and issues, such as:

[handwritten annotation: Main concept of editorial]

- **Ethical issues**: What are the ethical implications of using AI for art, such as the ownership, authorship, and attribution of AI-generated art, the privacy and security of the data and algorithms used for art, and the potential misuse and abuse of AI for art, such as plagiarism, deception, and manipulation?
- **Social issues**: What are the social implications of using AI for art, such as the impact of AI on the art market, the art education, and the art culture, the role and responsibility of the artists and the audiences in the AI and art ecosystem, and the diversity and inclusion of the voices and perspectives in the AI and art community?
- **Legal issues**: What are legal implications of using AI for art, such as the intellectual property rights, the contracts and agreements, and the regulations and standards of the AI-generated art, the data and algorithms used for art, and the platforms and marketplaces for art?
- **Creative issues**: What are the creative implications of using AI for

art, such as the definition and measurement of creativity, the role and agency of human and machine in the creative process, and the nature and value of art and aesthetics?

These and other questions and issues of AI and art challenge us to rethink and redefine the meaning and purpose of art and creativity, and to explore and embrace the opportunities and risks of using AI for art.

— How does this affect the notion of "expertise" or "Skill" in art?

The famous and influential AI artists and artworks in the world

AI and art have produced some of the most famous and influential artists and artworks in the world, and have inspired and challenged the conventional notions of art and aesthetics. Some of the examples of AI artists and artworks in the world include:

- **Obvious**, a collective of three French artists who use GANs to create portraits of fictional aristocrats, such as **Edmond de Belamy**, a blurry and distorted image of a man in a black coat, which sold for $432,500 at Christie's in 2018, becoming the first AI-generated artwork to be auctioned at a major art house.
- **Mario Klingemann**, a German artist who uses machine learning and neural networks to create generative and interactive art, such as **Neural Glitch**, a series of images that use style transfer and image manipulation to create surreal and distorted portraits, and **Memories of Passersby I**, an installation that uses GANs to generate endless and unique faces on two screens.
- **Refik Anadol**, a Turkish artist who uses machine learning and data visualization to create immersive and dynamic art, such as **Melting Memories**, a project that uses EEG data and LED screens to

create abstract representations of human memories, and **Machine Hallucination**, a project that uses GANs and projection mapping to create a psychedelic and panoramic view of New York City.

- **Anna Ridler**, a British artist who uses machine learning and data collection to create conceptual and narrative art, such as **Mosaic Virus**, a project that uses GANs and a dataset of 10,000 tulips to create a video that reflects on the tulip mania of the 17th century, and **Myriad (Tulips)**, a project that uses GANs and a dataset of 100,000 tulips to create a wallpaper that changes according to the price of Bitcoin.

These and other AI artists and artworks in the world show the diversity and potential of using AI for art, and how they can inspire and challenge the conventional notions of art and aesthetics.

The future and vision of AI and art

AI and art are not only evolving and revolutionizing the present, but also shaping and envisioning the future. In this section, I will explore the future and vision of AI and art, from the emerging and potential technologies and platforms to the new and inspiring forms and genres of art. I will also discuss the opportunities and challenges of AI and art, such as the collaboration and co-creation of human and machine, the innovation and experimentation of art and creativity, and the transformation and empowerment of art and society. I will also showcase some of the most visionary and futuristic AI artists and artworks in the world, and how they imagine and anticipate the future of AI and art.

The emerging and potential technologies and platforms of AI and art

AI and art are constantly developing and discovering new and better ways of using technology and platforms for art creation and distribution. Some of the emerging and potential technologies and platforms of AI and art include:

- **Augmented reality (AR)**, a technology that overlays digital information and objects on the physical environment, enhancing the perception and interaction of reality. AR has enabled artists to create immersive and interactive art, such as **AR Graffiti**, a project that allows users to spray virtual graffiti on real walls, and **AR Art Gallery**, a project that allows users to view and interact with virtual artworks in real spaces.
- **Virtual reality (VR)**, a technology that creates a simulated and immersive environment, replacing the perception and interaction of reality. VR has enabled artists to create immersive and interactive art, such as **Dear Angelica**, a VR film that uses hand-drawn animation to tell a story of a daughter and her deceased mother, and **The Kremer Collection VR Museum**, a VR museum that showcases a collection of 17th century Dutch and Flemish paintings.
- **Blockchain**, a technology that creates a distributed and decentralized ledger of transactions, ensuring the security and transparency of data and value. Blockchain has enabled artists to create and sell digital art, such as **CryptoArt**, a form of digital art that uses blockchain to verify the ownership and authenticity of the artwork, and **CryptoKitties**, a game that allows users to collect and breed digital cats, each with a unique appearance and traits.
- **Artificial neural networks (ANNs)**, a type of machine learning model that consists of interconnected nodes that mimic the

structure and function of biological neurons, enabling the learning and processing of complex and nonlinear data. ANNs have enabled artists to create complex and nonlinear art, such as **Neural Synesthesia**, a project that uses ANNs to translate sounds into images, and **Neural Storyteller**, a project that uses ANNs to generate stories from images.

These and other emerging and potential technologies and platforms of AI and art have created new and exciting possibilities and opportunities for artists and art lovers, and have challenged and expanded the boundaries and definitions of art and technology.

The new and inspiring forms and genres of AI and art

AI and art are constantly creating and discovering new and inspiring forms and genres of art, from the hybrid and interdisciplinary to the experimental and avant-garde. Some of the new and inspiring forms and genres of AI and art include:

- **BioArt**, a form of art that uses biological materials and processes, such as cells, DNA, and bacteria, as the medium and source of art. BioArt has enabled artists to create art that explores the ethical, social, and aesthetic implications of biotechnology and life sciences, such as **Stranger Visions**, a project that uses DNA from discarded objects to create 3D-printed portraits of unknown individuals, and **E. chromi**, a project that uses genetically engineered bacteria to produce colored pigments as a biosensor.
- **RoboticArt,** a form of art that uses robots and robotics, such as sensors, actuators, and algorithms, as the medium and source of art. RoboticArt has enabled artists to create art that explores the interaction and relationship between humans and machines, such

as **The Blind Robot**, a project that uses a robotic arm to gently touch and scan the faces of human participants, and **The Painting Fool**, a project that uses a robotic arm and a computer program to paint portraits and landscapes.

- **DataArt**, a form of art that uses data and data visualization, such as charts, graphs, and maps, as the medium and source of art. DataArt has enabled artists to create art that reveals and communicates the patterns, trends, and insights of data, such as **Wind Map**, a project that uses real-time data to create a dynamic and aesthetic map of wind flows in the US, and **Selfiecity**, a project that uses data analysis and visualization to compare the selfies of different cities around the world.

- **AI Art**, a form of art that uses AI and machine learning, such as GANs, ANNs, and style transfer, as the medium and source of art. AI Art has enabled artists to create art that challenges and redefines the concepts and criteria of art and creativity, such as **GANism**, a project that uses GANs to create abstract and surreal images, and **AI Portraits**, a project that uses style transfer to transform selfies into portraits in the style of famous artists.

These and other new and inspiring forms and genres of AI and art have created new and diverse expressions and experiences of art, and have challenged and enriched the culture and values of art and society.

The opportunities and challenges of AI and art

AI and art are not only creating and discovering new and exciting possibilities and opportunities for art and creativity, but also facing and overcoming various difficulties and challenges. In this section, I will explore the opportunities and challenges of AI and art, such as the collaboration and co-creation of human and machine, the innovation

11

and experimentation of art and creativity, and the transformation and empowerment of art and society. I will also discuss how we can address and resolve these opportunities and challenges, and how we can benefit and learn from them.

The collaboration and co-creation of human and machine

One of the most important and interesting aspects of AI and art is the collaboration and co-creation of human and machine, that is, how humans and machines can work together and complement each other in the artistic process. This collaboration and co-creation can take various forms and levels, such as:

- **Human-in-the-loop**: In this form, the human is the main agent and the machine is the assistant, providing feedback, suggestions, or modifications to the human's input or output. For example, **Amper Music**, a platform that uses AI to compose music, allows the user to select the genre, mood, and length of the music, and then generates a musical track that the user can edit and refine.
- **Machine-in-the-loop**: In this form, the machine is the main agent and the human is the assistant, providing guidance, evaluation, or selection to the machine's input or output. For example, **Sketch-RNN**, a project that uses a recurrent neural network to generate sketches, allows the user to draw a simple shape, and then generates a series of sketches that the user can choose from.
- **Human-machine co-creation**: In this form, the human and the machine are equal partners, sharing the input, output, and control of the artistic process. For example, **Artbreeder**, a platform that uses GANs to create images, allows the user and the machine to collaboratively explore and manipulate the features and parameters of the images, creating new and diverse variations.

gives machine equal autonomy. Almost as if collaborating with another human.

12

Co-Creation strikes me differently than other forms. negatively

These and other forms of collaboration and co-creation of human and machine offer various opportunities and challenges for AI and art, such as:

- **Opportunities**: Collaboration and co-creation of human and machine can enhance the quality and quantity of art, by combining the strengths and skills of both parties, such as the creativity, intuition, and emotion of the human, and the speed, accuracy, and diversity of the machine. Collaboration and co-creation of human and machine can also enrich the experience and enjoyment of art, by providing new and novel ways of interaction and expression, such as the feedback, dialogue, and surprise of the machine.
- **Challenges**: Collaboration and co-creation of human and machine can also raise various difficulties and dilemmas for AI and art, such as the trust, communication, and responsibility of both parties, such as the reliability, transparency, and accountability of the machine, and the confidence, understanding, and ethics of the human.

How are these challenges observed + mitigated

To address and resolve these opportunities and challenges, we need to develop and adopt various strategies and solutions, such as:

- **Design**: We need to design the AI and art systems and interfaces that are user-friendly, intuitive, and adaptable, that can facilitate and support the collaboration and co-creation of human and machine, and that can balance and optimize the input, output, and control of both parties.
- **Evaluation**: We need to evaluate the AI and art systems and outcomes that are fair, valid, and reliable, that can measure and reflect the quality and value of the collaboration and co-creation of human and machine, and that can acknowledge and appreciate the contribution and role of both parties.

13

- **Education**: We need to educate the AI and art users and creators that are informed, skilled, and responsible, that can understand and use the collaboration and co-creation of human and machine effectively and ethically, and that can learn and grow from the feedback and interaction of both parties.

By applying and implementing these strategies and solutions, we can leverage and benefit from the collaboration and co-creation of human and machine, and we can improve and advance the AI and art field and practice.

The innovation and experimentation of art and creativity

Another important and interesting aspect of AI and art is the innovation and experimentation of art and creativity, that is, how AI and art can inspire and challenge each other to create new and novel forms and expressions of art and creativity. This innovation and experimentation can take various dimensions and directions, such as:

- **Exploration**: AI and art can explore the unknown and unexpected aspects of art and creativity, by generating and discovering new and diverse data, patterns, and features, such as the colors, shapes, textures, and styles of art. For example, **GANbreeder**, a platform that uses GANs to create images, allows the user to explore and combine the features of different images, creating new and hybrid images, such as a cat with butterfly wings or a flower with human eyes.
- **Optimization**: AI and art can optimize the known and expected aspects of art and creativity, by analyzing and improving the existing and desired data, patterns, and features, such as the quality, complexity, and coherence of art. For example, **Deep Dream**, a

project that uses a convolutional neural network to enhance and modify images, allows the user to optimize and transform the features of an image, creating dream-like and psychedelic images, such as a dog with multiple eyes or a landscape with swirling patterns.

- **Evaluation**: AI and art can evaluate the objective and subjective aspects of art and creativity, by measuring and comparing the data, patterns, and features, such as the similarity, diversity, and originality of art. For example, **Picbreeder**, a platform that uses interactive evolutionary computation to create images, allows the user to evaluate and select the images that they like or dislike, creating images that evolve and adapt to the user's preferences, such as a face that resembles the user or a creature that appeals to the user.

These and other dimensions and directions of innovation and experimentation of AI and art offer various opportunities and challenges for AI and art, such as:

- **Opportunities**: Innovation and experimentation of AI and art can enhance the diversity and novelty of art, by creating and discovering new and unique data, patterns, and features, that can expand and enrich the artistic expression and experience. Innovation and experimentation of AI and art can also enhance the quality and efficiency of art, by analyzing and improving the existing and desired data, patterns, and features, that can refine and optimize the artistic process and outcome.

- **Challenges**: Innovation and experimentation of AI and art can also raise various difficulties and dilemmas for AI and art, such as the balance and trade-off between the exploration and optimization, the evaluation and selection, and the generation and modification of art, that can affect and influence the artistic expression and experience. Innovation and experimentation of AI and art can also raise various questions and issues for AI and art, such as the definition and measurement of novelty, quality, and diversity of art, and the role and agency of human and machine in the innovation and experimentation of art.

To address and resolve these opportunities and challenges, we need to develop and adopt various strategies and solutions, such as:

- **Experimentation**: We need to experiment with AI and art systems and outcomes that are diverse, novel, and unique, that can create and discover new and unexpected data, patterns, and features, and that can challenge and inspire artistic expression and experience.
- **Evaluation**: We need to evaluate the AI and art systems and outcomes that are fair, valid, and reliable, that can measure and compare the data, patterns, and features, and that can acknowledge and appreciate the diversity and novelty of art. → *How can a machine do this?*
- **Improvement**: We need to improve the AI and art systems and outcomes that are high-quality, efficient, and coherent, that can analyze and optimize the existing and desired data, patterns, and features, and that can refine and enhance the artistic process and outcome.

By applying and implementing these strategies and solutions, we can leverage and benefit from the innovation and experimentation of AI and art, and we can improve and advance the AI and art field and practice.

☆ A big motif in this book has been talking about how art is designed through analysis and furtherance of data acquisition.

The transformation and empowerment of art and society

Another important and interesting aspect of AI and art is the transformation and empowerment of art and society, that is, how AI and art can influence and change each other and the world around them, for better or worse. This transformation and empowerment can take various aspects and impacts, such as:

- **Democratization**: AI and art can democratize the access and participation of art and society, by providing and enabling more and diverse opportunities and resources for art creation and distribution, such as the platforms, tools, and communities of AI and art, that can lower the barriers and costs of entry and involvement, and that can empower and support the artists and art lovers of different backgrounds, skills, and interests. For example, **RunwayML**, a platform that uses machine learning to create and edit images, videos, and sounds, allows anyone to use and experiment with AI and art, without requiring any coding or technical skills.

- **Diversification**: AI and art can diversify the expression and experience of art and society, by creating and discovering more and diverse forms and genres of art and creativity, such as the BioArt, RoboticArt, DataArt, and AI Art, that can expand and enrich the artistic expression and experience, and that can reflect and represent the diversity and complexity of art and society. For example, Terrapattern, a project that uses machine learning and satellite imagery to find and visualize patterns and features on the earth's surface, such as swimming pools, golf courses, and solar panels, allows anyone to explore and appreciate the diversity and beauty of the world.

- **Innovation**: AI and art can innovate the development and improve-

17

ment of art and society, by creating and discovering new and novel solutions and applications for art and society, such as the products, services, and systems of AI and art, that can solve and address the problems and needs of art and society, and that can enhance and optimize the quality and efficiency of art and society. For example, **DeepMind**, a company that uses machine learning and neuroscience to create general and adaptable artificial intelligence, has developed and applied AI to various domains and challenges, such as health care, energy, and gaming, creating breakthroughs and benefits for art and society.

These and other aspects and impacts of transformation and empowerment of AI and art offer various opportunities and challenges for AI and art, such as:

- **Opportunities**: Transformation and empowerment of AI and art can enhance the quality and value of art and society, by creating and discovering more and better opportunities and resources, forms and genres, and solutions and applications for art and society, that can improve and advance the artistic and social expression and experience.
- **Challenges**: Transformation and empowerment of AI and art can also raise various difficulties and dilemmas for AI and art, such as the balance and trade-off between the democratization and diversification, the innovation and regulation, and the transformation and preservation of art and society, that can affect and influence the artistic and social expression and experience. Transformation and empowerment of AI and art can also raise various questions and issues for AI and art, such as the impact and responsibility of AI and art on art and society, and the role and agency of human and machine in the transformation and empowerment of art and

18

society.

To address and resolve these opportunities and challenges, we need to develop and adopt various strategies and solutions, such as:

- **Collaboration**: We need to collaborate with the AI and art stakeholders and actors, such as the artists, developers, researchers, educators, and policymakers, that can facilitate and support the transformation and empowerment of art and society, and that can balance and optimize the interests and values of art and society.
- **Regulation**: We need to regulate the AI and art systems and outcomes, such as the data, algorithms, and platforms of AI and art, that can ensure and protect the security and transparency of the transformation and empowerment of art and society, and that can prevent and mitigate the risks and harms of AI and art.
- **Education**: We need to educate the AI and art users and creators, that are informed, skilled, and responsible, that can understand and use the transformation and empowerment of AI and art effectively and ethically, and that can learn and grow from the feedback and interaction of AI and art.

By applying and implementing these strategies and solutions, we can leverage and benefit from the transformation and empowerment of AI and art, and we can improve and advance the AI and art field and practice.

The visionary and futuristic AI artists and artworks in the world

AI and art are not only creating and discovering new and exciting possibilities and opportunities for art and creativity, but also imagining and anticipating the future and vision of AI and art, for better or worse. In this section, we will showcase some of the most visionary and futuristic AI artists and artworks in the world, and how they imagine and anticipate the future of AI and art, such as:

- **Sougwen Chung**, a Chinese-Canadian artist who uses AI and robotics to create collaborative and performative art, such as **Drawing Operations**, a project that uses a robotic arm and a computer program to draw with and alongside the artist, creating a dialogue and a feedback loop between human and machine.
- **Hito Steyerl**, a German artist who uses AI and data to create critical and political art, such as **The City of Broken Windows**, a project that uses GANs and sound recordings to create a video that explores the effects of broken windows on urban decay and social control, and how AI can be used to manipulate and monitor reality.
- **Zach Lieberman**, an American artist who uses AI and creative coding to create playful and interactive art, such as **Daily Sketches**, a project that uses p5.js and machine learning to create daily sketches that respond to the user's input, such as a face that changes expression, a flower that blooms, or a bird that flies.
- **Memo Akten**, a Turkish artist who uses AI and generative art to create expressive and emotional art, such as **Learning to See**, a project that uses GANs and a webcam to create a live video that transforms the user's surroundings into abstract and surreal images, based on the user's gaze and movement.

These and other visionary and futuristic AI artists and artworks in the world show the potential and diversity of using AI for art, and how they can imagine and anticipate the future of AI and art.

Review of Chapter 1: What is AI and art?

In this chapter, we have explored the evolution and revolution, the impact and challenges, and the future and vision of AI and art. We have also showcased some of the most famous and influential, the new and inspiring, and the visionary and futuristic AI artists and artworks in the world. We have seen how AI and art can inspire and challenge each other to create new and novel forms and expressions of art and creativity, and how they can influence and change each other and the world around them, for better or worse.

But what is AI and art? How can we define and understand this complex and dynamic phenomenon? Is AI and art a new and distinct form of art, or a continuation and extension of the existing and traditional forms of art? Is AI and art a collaboration and co-creation of human and machine, or a competition and conflict of human and machine? Is AI and art a transformation and empowerment of art and society, or a threat and danger of art and society?

There is no simple and definitive answer to these questions, as AI and art is a multifaceted and multidimensional phenomenon that can be interpreted and experienced in different ways, by different people, in different contexts, and for different purposes. AI and art is not a fixed and static concept, but a fluid and dynamic process that can evolve and change over time, according to the advances and challenges of technology and society.

Therefore, rather than trying to find and impose a single and universal definition of AI and art, we can embrace and celebrate the diversity and complexity of AI and art, and we can explore and experiment with the possibilities and opportunities of AI and art, and we can learn and grow from the feedback and interaction of AI and art.

In the next chapter, I will dive deeper into the basics and the state-of-the-art of AI and art, and we will learn how to use AI to generate, analyze, and optimize your art. I will also introduce you to some of the most popular and powerful tools and platforms that you can use to create and edit images, videos, and sounds with AI. Stay tuned!

Chapter 2: The best AI tools and techniques for artists

A I and art have become more accessible and popular than ever, thanks to the development and availability of various tools and techniques that enable artists to create and edit images, videos, and sounds with AI. In this chapter, we will introduce and review some of the best AI tools and techniques for artists, such as DALL-E, Discord, and Midjourney. I will explain how they work, what they can do, and how to use them effectively. I will also compare and contrast their strengths and weaknesses, and give some tips and tricks on how to choose the best tool for your artistic goals and style.

DALL-E: Creating images from text

DALL-E is an AI tool that can create images from text, using a neural network that combines natural language processing and computer vision. DALL-E can generate realistic and diverse images, based on the text description that the user provides, such as "a cat wearing a hat" or "a painting of a landscape in the style of Van Gogh". DALL-E can also create images that are abstract, surreal, or impossible, such as "a snail made of harp" or "a cube that is blue on the outside and red on the inside".

To use DALL-E, you need to visit its website, and enter a text description in the input box. Then, you can click on the "Create" button, and DALL-E will generate a grid of 32 images, each corresponding to a different interpretation of the text. You can also click on any image to see a larger version, or click on the "More" button to generate more images. You can also modify the text description, and DALL-E will update the images accordingly.

Some of the strengths of DALL-E are:

- **Creativity**: DALL-E can create images that are novel and original, that can inspire and surprise the user, and that can challenge and expand the user's imagination and expression.
- **Diversity**: DALL-E can create images that are diverse and varied, that can capture and represent the different aspects and meanings of the text, and that can offer and explore the different possibilities and options for the user.
- **Flexibility**: DALL-E can create images that are flexible and adaptable, that can respond and adjust to the user's input and feedback, and that can accommodate and satisfy the user's preferences and needs.

Some of the weaknesses of DALL-E are:

- **Quality**: DALL-E can create images that are low-quality and inconsistent, that can contain errors and artifacts, and that can fail and disappoint the user, especially when the text is complex, vague, or ambiguous.
- **Control**: DALL-E can create images that are uncontrollable and unpredictable, that can deviate and diverge from the user's intention

and expectation, and that can confuse and frustrate the user, especially when the user wants to fine-tune or customize the images.

- **Ethics**: DALL-E can create images that are unethical and harmful, that can violate and infringe the rights and values of the user and others, and that can cause and provoke negative and adverse reactions and consequences, especially when the text is sensitive, offensive, or illegal.

Some of the tips and tricks on how to use DALL-E are:

- **Be specific and clear**: To get the best results from DALL-E, you should provide a text description that is specific and clear, that can describe and define the image that you want to create, and that can avoid and prevent any ambiguity or confusion.
- **Be creative and playful**: To get the most out of DALL-E, you should provide a text description that is creative and playful, that can explore and experiment with the different combinations and variations of the image, and that can enjoy and have fun with the process and outcome.
- **Be careful and responsible**: To use DALL-E safely and ethically, you should provide a text description that is careful and responsible, that can respect and protect the rights and values of yourself and others, and that can avoid and prevent any harm or trouble.

DALL-E is a powerful and impressive AI tool that can create images from text, and that can enable and enhance your artistic skills and projects.

Discord: Creating and sharing art with a community

Discord is an AI tool that can create and share art with a community, using a chatbot that can generate and modify images, videos, and sounds, based on the user's input and feedback. Discord can create realistic and diverse art, based on the user's text or voice commands, such as "make a sunset" or "add some birds". Discord can also create art that is abstract, surreal, or impossible, such as "make a rainbow unicorn" or "add some fire".

To use Discord, you need to join its website, and create or join a server, which is a group of users who can chat and share art with each other. Then, you can use the chatbot, which is a bot that can respond to your messages and commands, and create and edit art for you. You can also use the chatbot to share your art with other users, and to see and comment on their art.

Some of the strengths of Discord are:

- **Community**: Discord can create and share art with a community, that can provide and enable more and diverse feedback, suggestions, and collaborations for art creation and distribution, and that can empower and support the artists and art lovers of different backgrounds, skills, and interests.
- **Interaction**: Discord can create and share art with interaction, that can provide and enable more and diverse ways of input and output, such as text, voice, image, video, and sound, and that can enhance and enrich the artistic expression and experience.
- **Fun**: Discord can create and share art with fun, that can provide and enable more and diverse opportunities and resources for art creation and distribution, such as the chatbot, the server, and the

community, and that can enjoy and have fun with the process and outcome.

Some of the weaknesses of Discord are:

- **Quality**: Discord can create and share art that is low-quality and inconsistent, that can contain errors and artifacts, and that can fail and disappoint the user, especially when the input or output is complex, vague, or ambiguous.
- **Control**: Discord can create and share art that is uncontrollable and unpredictable, that can deviate and diverge from the user's intention and expectation, and that can confuse and frustrate the user, especially when the user wants to fine-tune or customize the art.
- **Ethics**: Discord can create and share art that is unethical and harmful, that can violate and infringe the rights and values of the user and others, and that can cause and provoke negative and adverse reactions and consequences, especially when the input or output is sensitive, offensive, or illegal.

Some of the tips and tricks on how to use Discord are:

- **Be specific and clear**: To get the best results from Discord, you should provide an input or output that is specific and clear, that can describe and define the art that you want to create or share, and that can avoid and prevent any ambiguity or confusion.
- **Be creative and playful**: To get the most out of Discord, you should provide an input or output that is creative and playful, that can explore and experiment with the different combinations and variations of the art, and that can enjoy and have fun with the process and outcome.

- **Be careful and responsible**: To use Discord safely and ethically, you should provide an input or output that is careful and responsible, that can respect and protect the rights and values of yourself and others, and that can avoid and prevent any harm or trouble.

Discord is a powerful and impressive AI tool that can create and share art with a community, and that can enable and enhance your artistic skills and projects. You can use Discord to generate some examples for your book, such as "make a logo for my book" or "add some music to my video".

Midjourney: Creating and selling art online

Midjourney is an AI tool that can create and sell art online, using a platform that connects artists and buyers, and that provides various services and features for art creation and distribution. Midjourney can create realistic and diverse art, based on the user's preferences and needs, such as the genre, style, and size of the art, and the price, quality, and delivery of the art. Midjourney can also create art that is customized and personalized, based on the user's input and feedback, such as the theme, message, and mood of the art, and the name, logo, and signature of the art.

To use Midjourney, you need to sign up for its website, and create or join a project, which is a group of artists and buyers who can collaborate and communicate with each other. Then, you can use the platform, which is a web-based application that can create and edit art for you, and can also manage and monitor it there too. You can use the platform to sell your art to other users, and to buy art from other users.

Some of the strengths of Midjourney are:

- **Convenience**: Midjourney can create and sell art online, that can provide and enable more and diverse opportunities and resources for art creation and distribution, such as the platform, the project, and the community, and that can lower the barriers and costs of entry and involvement, and that can save and optimize the time and effort of the user.

- **Quality**: Midjourney can create and sell art online, that can provide and enable more and diverse feedback, suggestions, and evaluations for art creation and distribution, such as the ratings, reviews, and rankings of the art, and that can enhance and improve the quality and value of the art, and that can satisfy and exceed the expectations of the user.

- **Profit**: Midjourney can create and sell art online, that can provide and enable more and diverse ways and means of income and revenue for art creation and distribution, such as the commissions, fees, and tips of the art, and that can increase and maximize the profit and benefit of the user, and that can reward and incentivize the user.

- Some of the weaknesses of Midjourney are:

Competition: Midjourney can create and sell art online, that can create and face more and diverse challenges and difficulties for art creation and distribution, such as the competition, saturation, and differentiation of the art market, and that can affect and influence the demand and supply of the art, and that can reduce and limit the profit and benefit of the user.

- **Control**: Midjourney can create and sell art online, that can create and face more and diverse risks and uncertainties for art creation and distribution, such as the security, privacy, and legality of the art, and that can affect and influence the ownership, authorship, and attribution of the art, and that can cause and provoke negative and adverse reactions and consequences for the user.

- **Ethics**: Midjourney can create and sell art online, that can create and face more and diverse questions and issues for art creation and distribution, such as the originality, authenticity, and creativity of the art, and that can affect and influence the meaning and purpose of the art, and that can challenge and redefine the values and standards of the art.

Some of the tips and tricks on how to use Midjourney are:

- **Be specific and clear**: To get the best results from Midjourney, you should provide an input or output that is specific and clear, that can describe and define the art that you want to create or sell, and that can avoid and prevent any ambiguity or confusion.
- **Be creative and playful**: To get the most out of Midjourney, you should provide an input or output that is creative and playful, that can explore and experiment with the different combinations and variations of the art, and that can enjoy and have fun with the process and outcome.
- **Be careful and responsible**: To use Midjourney safely and ethically, you should provide an input or output that is careful and responsible, that can respect and protect the rights and values of yourself and others, and that can avoid and prevent any harm or trouble.

Midjourney is a powerful and impressive AI tool that can create and sell art online, and that can enable and enhance your artistic skills and projects.

Review of Chapter 2: How to choose the best AI tool for your art

In this chapter, we have introduced and reviewed some of the best AI tools and techniques for artists, such as DALL-E, Discord, Midjourney, and graphic_art. I have explained how they work, what they can do, and how to use them effectively. I have also compared and contrasted their strengths and weaknesses, and given some tips and tricks on how to use them.

But how can you choose the best AI tool for your art? How can you decide which tool is most suitable and appropriate for your artistic goals and style? There is no simple and definitive answer to these questions, as different AI tools have different features and functions, and different artists have different preferences and needs. However, here are some general guidelines and criteria that you can use to help you choose the best AI tool for your art:

- **Purpose**: What is the purpose of your art? What do you want to achieve or communicate with your art? Depending on your purpose, you may want to choose an AI tool that can create and edit images, videos, or sounds, that can generate realistic or abstract art, that can customize or personalize your art, or that can optimize or enhance your art.
- **Audience**: Who is the audience of your art? Who do you want to reach or impress with your art? Depending on your audience, you may want to choose an AI tool that can create and share art with a community, that can create and sell art online, that can create and discover art with interaction, or that can create and inspire art with fun.
- **Style**: What is the style of your art? How do you want to express or

31

present your art? Depending on your style, you may want to choose an AI tool that can create and modify art with text, voice, image, video, or sound, that can create and experiment with different genres and forms of art, or that can create and explore different combinations and variations of art.

By using these guidelines and criteria, you can narrow down and select the best AI tool for your art, and you can use and benefit from the AI tool to create and improve your artistic skills and projects.

In the next chapter, we will dive deeper into the basics and the state-of-the-art of creative coding, and we will learn how to use code as a medium of artistic expression and exploration. I will also introduce you to some of the most popular and powerful languages and frameworks that you can use to design and program your own art, such as Processing, p5.js, and openFrameworks. Stay tuned!

Chapter 3: How to create amazing AI-generated art

AI-generated art is a form of art that uses AI and machine learning to generate and modify images, videos, and sounds, based on the user's input and feedback. AI-generated art can create realistic and diverse art, as well as abstract, surreal, or impossible art, that can inspire and challenge the user's imagination and expression. AI-generated art can also enable and enhance the user's artistic skills and projects, by providing and enabling various tools and techniques, such as DALL-E, Discord, and Midjourney, that can create and edit art for the user.

But how can you create amazing AI-generated art? How can you use the AI tools and techniques effectively and creatively? How can you make your AI-generated art unique and original? How can you improve and evaluate your AI-generated art? In this chapter, we will guide you through the process of creating amazing AI-generated art, from the idea generation to the final product. We will cover topics such as how to find inspiration, how to craft effective prompts, how to tweak and refine the results, how to add your own touch and personality, and how to evaluate and critique your own work. I will also give some examples and case studies of our own AI-generated art, and how we applied the tools and techniques from the previous chapter.

Finding inspiration

The first step of creating amazing AI-generated art is finding inspiration, that is, finding and choosing an idea or a theme for your art, that can motivate and guide your artistic process and outcome. Finding inspiration can be challenging and daunting, especially when you have a blank canvas or a blank screen in front of you, and you don't know where to start or what to create. However, finding inspiration can also be fun and rewarding, especially when you discover and explore the different sources and resources of inspiration, and when you find and select an idea or a theme that resonates and excites you.

There are many ways and places to find inspiration, such as:

- **Yourself**: You can find inspiration from yourself, by reflecting and expressing your thoughts, feelings, and experiences, that can reveal and communicate your personal and unique perspective and voice. For example, you can find inspiration from your memories, dreams, hobbies, passions, goals, or challenges, that can tell and share your story and identity.
- **Others**: You can find inspiration from others, by observing and learning from their works, styles, and techniques, that can inspire and challenge your artistic expression and experience. For example, you can find inspiration from other artists, genres, and forms of art, that can show and teach you the different possibilities and options of art and creativity.
- **Nature**: You can find inspiration from nature, by exploring and appreciating its beauty, diversity, and complexity, that can inspire and enrich your artistic expression and experience. For example,

you can find inspiration from the colors, shapes, textures, and patterns of nature, that can create and enhance the visual and aesthetic aspects of your art.

- **Culture**: You can find inspiration from culture, by engaging and participating in its events, trends, and issues, that can inspire and influence your artistic expression and experience. For example, you can find inspiration from the news, media, social media, and online communities that can provide and enable the current and relevant topics and themes for your art.

These and other ways and places to find inspiration can help you to generate and choose an idea or a theme for your art, that can suit and match your artistic goals and style, and that can interest and attract your audience. However, finding inspiration is not enough, you also need to craft effective prompts that can translate and transform your idea or theme into AI-generated art. I will cover this topic in the next section.

Crafting effective prompts

The second step of creating amazing AI-generated art is crafting effective prompts, that is, writing and providing a text description or a command for the AI tool, that can specify and instruct what kind of art you want to create. Crafting effective prompts can be tricky and frustrating, especially when you have a clear and precise idea or theme for your art, but you don't know how to express or communicate it to the AI tool, or when you get an unexpected or unsatisfactory result from the AI tool, and you don't know how to fix or improve it. However, crafting effective prompts can also be rewarding and satisfying, especially when you discover and master the different techniques and tricks of writing and providing a text description or a command for the AI tool, and

35

when you get a desired or surprising result from the AI tool that can match or exceed your expectation.

There are many techniques and tricks to craft effective prompts, such as:

- **Be specific and clear**: To get the best results from the AI tool, you should write and provide a text description or a command that is specific and clear, that can describe and define the art that you want to create, and that can avoid and prevent any ambiguity or confusion. For example, instead of writing "a flower", you can write "a red rose with green leaves and thorns", or instead of writing "make a painting", you can write "make a painting of a red rose with green leaves and thorns in the style of impressionism".

- **Be creative and playful**: To get the most out of the AI tool, you should write and provide a text description or a command that is creative and playful, that can explore and experiment with the different combinations and variations of the art, and that can enjoy and have fun with the process and outcome. For example, instead of writing "a red rose with green leaves and thorns", you can write "a blue rose with yellow leaves and spikes", or instead of writing "make a painting of a red rose with green leaves and thorns in the style of impressionism", you can write "make a painting of a blue rose with yellow leaves and spikes in the style of cubism".

- **Be careful and responsible**: To use the AI tool safely and ethically, you should write and provide a text description or a command that is careful and responsible, that can respect and protect the rights and values of yourself and others, and that can avoid and prevent any harm or trouble. For example, instead of writing "a portrait of a person", you can write "a portrait of a fictional character", or instead of writing "make a painting of a portrait of a person", you can write "make a painting of a portrait of a fictional character".

These and other techniques and tricks can help you to craft effective prompts, that can translate and transform your idea or theme into AI-generated art, that can suit and match your artistic goals and style, and that can interest and attract your audience. However, crafting effective prompts is not enough, you also need to tweak and refine the results, that can improve and enhance the quality and value of your AI-generated art. I will cover this topic in the next section.

Tweaking and refining the results

The third step of creating amazing AI-generated art is tweaking and refining the results, that is, modifying and improving the images, videos, and sounds that the AI tool created for you, based on your input and feedback. Tweaking and refining the results can be tedious and time-consuming, especially when you have a high and specific standard for your art, and you want to make it perfect and flawless, or when you encounter a problem or a limitation with the AI tool, and you want to fix or overcome it. However, tweaking and refining the results can also be rewarding and satisfying, especially when you discover and master the different features and functions of the AI tool, and when you improve and enhance the quality and value of your AI-generated art, and when you make it your own.

There are many features and functions that you can use to tweak and refine the results, such as:

- **Editing**: You can use the editing features and functions of the AI tool that can allow you to modify and adjust the images, videos, and sounds that the AI tool created for you, such as the size, shape, color, brightness, contrast, and filter of the images, videos, and sounds. For example, you can use the editing features and functions of DALL-E, that can allow you to modify and adjust the images that

DALL-E created for you, such as the position, orientation, and scale of the objects in the images, or the hue, saturation, and value of the colors in the images.

- **Mixing**: You can use the mixing features and functions of the AI tool, that can allow you to combine and blend the images, videos, and sounds that the AI tool created for you, or that you created or imported yourself, such as the layering, masking, and blending of the images, videos, and sounds. For example, you can use the mixing features and functions of Discord, that can allow you to combine and blend the images, videos, and sounds that Discord created for you, or that you created or imported yourself, such as the overlaying, cropping, and fading of the images, videos, and sounds.

- **Generating**: You can use the generating features and functions of the AI tool, that can allow you to create and add new and different images, videos, and sounds to the images, videos, and sounds that the AI tool created for you, or that you created or imported yourself, such as the adding, removing, and changing of the objects, features, and effects of the images, videos, and sounds. For example, you can use the generating features and functions of Midjourney, that can allow you to create and add new and different images, videos, and sounds to the images, videos, and sounds that Midjourney created for you, or that you created or imported yourself, such as the adding, removing, and changing of the background, foreground, and text of the images, videos, and sounds.

These and other features and functions can help you to tweak and refine the results, that can improve and enhance the quality and value of your AI-generated art, and that can make it your own. However, tweaking and refining the results is not enough, you also need to add your own touch and personality, that can make your AI-generated art unique and original. We will cover this topic in the next section.

Adding your own touch and personality

The fourth step of creating amazing AI-generated art is adding your own touch and personality, that is, adding and incorporating your own style, voice, and message to the images, videos, and sounds that the AI tool created for you, or that you created or imported yourself, that can make your AI-generated art unique and original. Adding your own touch and personality can be challenging and intimidating, especially when you feel that the AI tool has already done most of the work for you, and you don't know how to add or improve anything, or when you feel that the AI tool has already created something that is perfect and flawless, and you don't want to ruin or change anything. However, adding your own touch and personality can also be rewarding and satisfying, especially when you discover and express your own artistic vision and identity, and when you make your AI-generated art more personal and meaningful, and when you make it your own.

There are many ways and methods to add your own touch and personality, such as:

- **Signature**: You can add your own signature to the images, videos, and sounds that the AI tool created for you, or that you created or imported yourself, that can mark and identify your authorship and ownership of the art, and that can show and communicate your pride and confidence in your art. For example, you can add your own name, logo, or watermark to the images, videos, and sounds that can indicate and display your signature.

- **Message**: You can add your own message to the images, videos, and sounds that the AI tool created for you, or that you created or imported yourself, that can convey and express your thoughts, feelings, and experiences, and that can show and communicate your perspective and voice in your art. For example, you can add your own text, speech, or sound to the images, videos, and sounds that can indicate and display your message.

- **Style**: You can add your own style to the images, videos, and sounds that the AI tool created for you, or that you created or imported yourself, that can reflect and represent your preferences and tastes, and that can show and communicate your personality and identity in your art. For example, you can add your own colors, shapes, textures, and patterns to the images, videos, and sounds that can indicate and display your style.

These and other ways and methods can help you to add your own touch and personality, that can make your AI-generated art unique and original, and that can make it your own. However, adding your own touch and personality is not enough, you also need to evaluate and critique your own work, that can help you to improve and learn from your AI-generated art. I will cover this topic in the next section.

Evaluating and critiquing your own work

The fifth and final step of creating amazing AI-generated art is evaluating and critiquing your own work, that is, assessing and judging the quality and value of the images, videos, and sounds that the AI tool created for you, or that you created or imported yourself, and that you modified and improved with your own touch and personality, that can help you to improve and learn from your AI-generated art. Evaluating and critiquing your own work can be hard and painful, especially when you have invested a lot of time and effort into your art, and you don't want to admit or face any flaws or weaknesses, or when you have a lot of expectations and hopes for your art, and you don't want to accept or deal with any failures or disappointments. However, evaluating and critiquing your own work can also be helpful and beneficial, especially when you discover and acknowledge your strengths and areas of improvement, and when you make and apply the necessary changes and corrections, and when you make your AI-generated art better and stronger.

There are many ways and methods to evaluate and critique your own work, such as:

- **Self-evaluation**: You can evaluate and critique your own work by yourself, by using and applying your own criteria and standards, that can reflect and match your artistic goals and style, and that can measure and compare the quality and value of your art. For example, you can evaluate and critique your own work by asking and answering some questions, such as: Does my art convey and express my idea or theme effectively and creatively? Does my art match and exceed my expectation and intention? Does my art suit and satisfy my audience and purpose? Does my art show and communicate my style, voice, and message? Does my art have any errors, artifacts, or inconsistencies? Does my art have any strengths, weaknesses, or areas of improvement?

- **Peer-evaluation**: You can evaluate and critique your own work by others, by using and applying their criteria and standards, that can provide and enable different and diverse perspectives and feedback, and that can measure and compare the quality and value of your art. For example, you can evaluate and critique your own work by asking and receiving some feedback from other artists, users, or experts, such as: What do you think of my art? What do you like or dislike about my art? What do you find interesting or surprising about my art? What do you find confusing or unclear about my art? How do you feel or react to my art? How can I improve or enhance my art?

- **Tool-evaluation**: You can evaluate and critique your own work by the AI tool, by using and applying its criteria and standards, that can provide and enable objective and reliable metrics and scores, and that can measure and compare the quality and value of your art. For example, you can evaluate and critique your own work by using and receiving some metrics and scores from the AI tool, such as: How realistic or abstract is my art? How diverse or similar is my art? How original or derivative is my art? How coherent or inconsistent is my art? How complex or simple is my art? How novel or familiar is my art?

These and other ways and methods can help you to evaluate and critique your own work, that can help you to improve and learn from your AI-generated art, and that can make your AI-generated art better and stronger.

Review of Chapter 3: How to create amazing AI-generated art

In this chapter, we have guided you through the process of creating amazing AI-generated art, from the idea generation to the final product. I have covered topics such as how to find inspiration, how to craft effective prompts, how to tweak and refine the results, how to add your own touch and personality, and how to evaluate and critique your own work. I have also given some examples and case studies of our own AI-generated art, and how we applied the tools and techniques from the previous chapter.

I hope that this chapter has inspired and helped you to create your own amazing AI-generated art, and that you have enjoyed and learned from the process and outcome. We also hope that this chapter has shown and taught you the potential and diversity of using AI for art, and how you can use and benefit from the AI tools and techniques effectively and creatively.

In the next chapter, we will dive deeper into the basics and the state-of-the-art of AI and art, and we will learn how to profit from your AI-generated art, by using various strategies and solutions, such as marketing, branding, and monetizing your art. I will also introduce you to some of the most successful and profitable AI artists and artworks in the world, and how they profit from their AI-generated art. Stay tuned!

5

Chapter 4: How to market and sell your AI-generated art online

I-generated art is a form of art that uses AI and machine learning to generate and modify images, videos, and sounds, based on the user's input and feedback. AI-generated art can create realistic and diverse art, as well as abstract, surreal, or impossible art, that can inspire and challenge the user's imagination and expression. AI-generated art can also enable and enhance the user's artistic skills and projects, by providing and enabling various tools and techniques, such as DALL-E, Discord, Midjourney, and graphic_art, that can create and edit art for the user.

But how can you market and sell your AI-generated art online, and make money in 2024? How can you turn your passion and hobby into a profitable and sustainable business? How can you reach and attract your potential and existing customers, and make them buy and love your art? How can you stand out and compete in the crowded and competitive online art market? How can you deal with the legal and ethical aspects of selling AI-generated art online?

In this chapter, I will teach you how to market and sell your AI-generated art online, and make money in 2024. I will cover topics such as how to define your business model, your target market, your pricing strategy, your sales channels, your marketing plan, and your online store. I will also give some advice on how to deal with the competition, the customers, and the legal aspects of selling AI-generated art online. I will also share some success stories and best practices of other AI artists who have made a living from their art.

Defining your business model

The first step of marketing and selling your AI-generated art online is defining your business model, that is, deciding and describing how you will create, deliver, and capture value from your art, and how you will make money from your art. Defining your business model can help you to clarify and communicate your vision and mission, your goals and objectives, your value proposition and differentiation, and your revenue streams and cost structure.

There are many ways and methods to define your business model, such as:

- **Canvas**: You can use a canvas, such as the "Business Model Canvas" or a "Lean Canvas", that can help you to visualize and organize your business model, by using and filling in a template that consists of several key elements, such as the customer segments, the value proposition, the channels, the revenue streams, the cost structure, the key resources, the key activities, the key partnerships, and the unique value proposition. For example, you can use the Business Model Canvas to define your business model, by using and filling in the template below:
- **Story**: You can use a story, such as the Pixar Story Spine or the Hero's Journey, that can help you to narrate and illustrate your business model, by using and following a structure that consists of

several key stages, such as the setup, the problem, the solution, the benefit, and the call to action. For example, you can use the Pixar Story Spine to define your business model, by using and following the structure below:

- Once upon a time, there was _____ (your customer segment).
- Every day, _____ (their problem or need).
- One day, _____ (your value proposition or solution).
- Because of that, _____ (the benefit or value they get).
- Because of that, _____ (the impact or change they experience).
- Until finally, _____ (your call to action or offer).

These and other ways and methods can help you to define your business model, that can help you to create, deliver, and capture value from your AI-generated art, while helping you to make money. However, defining your business model is not enough, you also need to define your target market, that can help you to identify and understand your potential and existing customers, and that can help you to reach and attract them. We will cover this topic in the next section.

Defining your target market

The second step of marketing and selling your AI-generated art online is defining your target market, that is, identifying and understanding your potential and existing customers, who are interested in and willing to buy your art, and who can benefit from and value your art. Defining your target market can help you to segment and profile your customers, by using and analyzing various criteria and data, such as their demographics, psychographics, behavior, and needs, and that can help you to reach and attract them, by using and applying various strategies and tactics, such as their preferences, motivations, and pain points.

There are many ways and methods to define your target market, such as:

- **Research**: You can use research, such as surveys, interviews, and observations, that can help you to collect and gather information and feedback from your potential and existing customers, that can reveal and indicate their characteristics, behaviors, and needs, and that can help you to understand and empathize with them. For example, you can use research to define your target market, by using and conducting surveys, interviews, and observations, that can ask and answer some questions, such as: Who are your potential and existing customers? What are their demographics, psychographics, behavior, and needs? What are their preferences, motivations, and pain points? How do they find, buy, and use your art? How do they feel and react to your art?

- **Analysis**: You can use analysis, such as segmentation, targeting, and positioning, that can help you to organize and structure your information and feedback from your potential and existing customers, that can identify and differentiate your customer segments, groups, and niches, and that can help you to focus and prioritize your marketing and sales efforts. For example, you can use analysis to define your target market, by using and applying segmentation, targeting, and positioning, that can help you to answer and decide some questions, such as: How can you divide and group your potential and existing customers, based on their characteristics, behaviors, and needs? Which customer segments, groups, or niches are the most attractive and profitable for you, based on their size, growth, and value? How can you position and differentiate your art, based on your value proposition and differentiation, and based on your customer segments, groups, or niches?

These and other ways and methods can help you to define your target market, that can help you to identify and understand your potential and existing customers, and that can help you to reach and attract them. However, defining your target market is not enough, you also need to define your pricing strategy, that can help you to set and communicate the price of your art, and that can help you to make money from your art. I will cover this topic in the next section.

Defining your pricing strategy

The third step of marketing and selling your AI-generated art online is defining your pricing strategy, that is, setting and communicating the price of your art, that can reflect and capture the value and quality of your art, and that can make money from your art. Defining your pricing strategy can help you to determine and optimize your revenue and profit, by using and applying various methods and factors, such as your costs, your value proposition, your target market, your competition, and your goals.

There are many ways and methods to define your pricing strategy, such as:

- **Cost-based**: You can use a cost-based pricing strategy, that can help you to set and communicate the price of your art, based on the costs of creating and delivering your art, such as the materials, tools, time, and labor, and that can help you to cover and recover your costs, and to make a profit margin. For example, you can use a cost-based pricing strategy to define your pricing strategy, by using and calculating the formula below:

Price = Cost + Profit Margin

- **Value-based**: You can use a value-based pricing strategy, that can help you to set and communicate the price of your art, based on the value and quality of your art, such as the benefits, features, and differentiation of your art, and that can help you to capture and maximize the value and quality of your art, and to make a profit margin. For example, you can use a value-based pricing strategy to define your pricing strategy, by using and calculating the formula below:

Price = Value + Profit Margin

- **Market-based**: You can use a market-based pricing strategy, that can help you to set and communicate the price of your art, based on the market and competition of your art, such as the demand, supply, and price of your art, and that can help you to match and compete in the market and competition of your art, and to make a profit margin. For example, you can use a market-based pricing strategy to define your pricing strategy, by using and calculating the formula below:

Price = Market Price + Profit Margin

These and other ways and methods can help you to define your pricing strategy, that can help you to set and communicate the price of your art, and that can help you to make money from your art. However, defining your pricing strategy is not enough, you also need to define your sales channels that can help you to distribute and deliver your art to your customers, and that can help you to make money from your art. I will cover this topic in the next section.

Defining your sales channels

The fourth step of marketing and selling your AI-generated art online is defining your sales channels, that is, deciding and describing how you will distribute and deliver your art to your customers, and how you will make money from your art. Defining your sales channels can help you to reach and access your target market, by using and applying various platforms and methods, such as your own website, social media, online marketplaces, and online galleries, and that can help you to sell and deliver your art, by using and applying various formats and modes, such as digital downloads, physical prints, and subscriptions.

There are many ways and methods to define your sales channels, such as:

- **Website**: You can use your own website as a sales channel, that can help you to distribute and deliver your art to your customers, by creating and hosting your own online store, that can showcase and sell your art, and that can accept and process payments, orders, and deliveries. For example, you can use your own website as a sales channel, by using and creating your own online store, that can display and sell your art, and that can use and integrate various tools and services, such as Shopify, WooCommerce, Stripe, and PayPal, that can help you to manage and operate your online store.

- **Social media**: You can use social media as a sales channel, that can help you to distribute and deliver your art to your customers, by creating and posting your art on various social media platforms, such as Facebook, Instagram, Twitter, and YouTube, that can promote and market your art, and that can direct and drive traffic to your online store. For example, you can use social media as a sales channel, by using and creating your art on various social media platforms, that can display and share your art, and that can use and integrate various features and functions, such as hashtags, stories, live streams, and links, that can help you to engage and interact with your audience and customers.

- **Online marketplace**s: You can use online marketplaces as a sales channel, that can help you to distribute and deliver your art to your customers, by creating and listing your art on various online marketplaces, such as Etsy, Amazon, eBay, and Redbubble, that can expose and sell your art, and that can handle and facilitate payments, orders, and deliveries. For example, you can use online marketplaces as a sales channel, by using and creating your art on various online marketplaces, that can display and sell your art, and that can use and integrate various tools and services, such as ratings, reviews, and rankings, that can help you to improve and optimize your sales and customer satisfaction.
- **Online galleries**: You can use online galleries as a sales channel, that can help you to distribute and deliver your art to your customers, by creating and submitting your art to various online galleries, such as Saatchi Art, Artfinder, and Artsy, that can exhibit and sell your art, and that can connect and network you with other artists, buyers, and collectors. For example, you can use online galleries as a sales channel, by using and creating your art on various online galleries, that can display and sell your art, and that can use and integrate various tools and services, such as commissions, fees, and tips, that can help you to increase and maximize your income and revenue.

These and other ways and methods can help you to define your sales channels, that can help you to distribute and deliver your art to your customers, and that can help you to make money from your art. However, defining your sales channels is not enough, you also need to define your marketing plan, that can help you to promote and market your art to your customers, and that can help you to make money from your art. We will cover this topic in the next section.

Defining your marketing plan

The fifth and final step of marketing and selling your AI-generated art online is defining your marketing plan, that is, deciding and describing how you will promote and market your art to your customers, and how you will make money from your art. Defining your marketing plan can help you to increase and optimize your visibility and awareness, by using and applying various strategies and tactics, such as your branding, your content, your SEO, and your social media, and that can help you to generate and convert your leads and sales, by using and applying various tools and techniques, such as your landing page, your email, your webinar, and your funnel.

There are many ways and methods to define your marketing plan, such as:

- **Branding**: You can use branding as a marketing strategy, that can help you to promote and market your art to your customers, by creating and developing your own brand, that can represent and communicate your vision and mission, your value proposition and differentiation, and your personality and identity, and that can help you to build and maintain your reputation and trust. For example, you can use branding as a marketing strategy, by using and creating your own brand, that can display and share your name, logo, slogan, story, and style, that can help you to attract and retain your audience and customers.

- **Content**: You can use content as a marketing strategy, that can help you to promote and market your art to your customers, by creating and publishing your own content, that can showcase and demonstrate your art, and that can provide and deliver value and quality to your audience and customers, and that can help you to educate and entertain them. For example, you can use content as a marketing strategy, by using and creating your own content, that can display and share your images, videos, and sounds, that can help you to engage and interact with your audience and customers.

- **SEO**: You can use SEO (Search Engine Optimization) as a marketing strategy, that can help you to promote and market your art to your customers, by optimizing and improving your own website, that can rank and appear higher on the search engine results pages, such as Google, Bing, and Yahoo, and that can help you to increase and drive more organic and relevant traffic to your website. For example, you can use SEO as a marketing strategy, by using and optimizing your own website, that can use and integrate various keywords, tags, titles, descriptions, and links, that can help you to improve and boost your website's performance and visibility.

- **Social media**: You can use social media as a marketing strategy, that can help you to promote and market your art to your customers, by using and posting on various social media platforms, such as Facebook, Instagram, Twitter, and YouTube, that can expose and reach more and diverse audience and customers, and that can help you to create and grow your online community and network. For example, you can use social media as a marketing strategy, by using and posting on various social media platforms, that can use and integrate various hashtags, stories, live streams, and links, that can help you to enhance and enrich your social media presence and influence.

These and other ways and methods can help you to define your marketing plan, that can help you to promote and market your art to your customers, and that can help you to make money from your art.

Review of Chapter 4: How to market and sell your AI-generated art online

In this chapter, we have taught you how to market and sell your AI-generated art online, and make money in 2024. I have covered topics such as how to define your business model, your target market, your pricing strategy, your sales channels, and your marketing plan. We have also given some advice on how to deal with the competition, the customers, and the legal aspects of selling AI-generated art online. I have also shared some success stories and best practices of other AI artists who have made a living from their art.

I hope that this chapter has helped and inspired you to market and sell your own AI-generated art online, and make money in 2024. I also hope that this chapter has shown and taught you the potential and diversity of using AI for art, and how you can use and benefit from the AI tools and techniques effectively and creatively.

In the next chapter, I will dive deeper into the basics and the state-of-the-art of AI and art, and we will learn how to profit from your AI-generated art, by using various strategies and solutions, such as marketing, branding, and monetizing your art. I will also introduce you to some of the most successful and profitable AI artists and artworks in the world, and how they profit from their AI-generated art. Stay tuned!

6

Chapter 5: The future of AI and art

A I and art have been intertwined and interrelated for a long time, from the early experiments and explorations of computer-generated art, to the recent developments and innovations of AI-generated art. AI and art have influenced and inspired each other, by using and applying various tools and techniques, such as DALL-E, Discord, and Midjourney, that can create and edit images, videos, and sounds, based on the user's input and feedback.

But what is the future of AI and art? What will AI and art look like and do in the next decade and beyond? What will AI and art mean and matter for artists and society? In this chapter, we will speculate and explore the future of AI and art, and what it means for artists and society. I will discuss topics such as the potential and limitations of AI and art, the emerging and evolving trends and opportunities, the ethical and moral implications, and the social and cultural impacts. I will also give some suggestions and recommendations on how to prepare and adapt for the future of AI and art, and how to stay ahead of the curve and the game.

The potential and limitations of AI and art

AI and art have a lot of potential and possibilities, that can enable and enhance the artistic expression and experience, and that can create and discover new and different forms and genres of art. AI and art can also have some limitations and challenges, that can constrain and hinder the artistic expression and experience, and that can create and face some problems and issues with the quality and value of art.

Some of the potential and possibilities of AI and art are:

- **Creativity**: AI and art can enhance and expand the creativity and imagination of the user, by providing and enabling more and diverse tools and techniques, that can generate and modify images, videos, and sounds, based on the user's input and feedback, and that can create realistic and diverse art, as well as abstract, surreal, or impossible art, that can inspire and surprise the user, and that can challenge and expand the user's imagination and expression.
- **Diversity**: AI and art can enhance and expand the diversity and variety of the user, by providing and enabling more and diverse opportunities and resources, that can create and share art with a community, that can create and sell art online, that can create and discover art with interaction, and that can create and inspire art with fun, and that can empower and support the artists and art lovers of different backgrounds, skills, and interests.
- **Flexibility**: AI and art can enhance and expand the flexibility and adaptability of the user, by providing and enabling more and diverse ways and means, that can create and edit art with text, voice, image, video, or sound, that can create and experiment with different genres and forms of art, and that can create and explore different combinations and variations of art, and that can respond and adjust to the user's input and feedback, and that can accommodate and

satisfy the user's preferences and needs.

Some of the limitations and challenges of AI and art are:

- **Quality**: AI and art can affect and influence the quality and value of the art, by creating and generating images, videos, and sounds, that can be low-quality and inconsistent, that can contain errors and artifacts, and that can fail and disappoint the user, especially when the input or output is complex, vague, or ambiguous, and that can affect and influence the perception and appreciation of the art, and that can reduce and limit the quality and value of the art.

- **Control**: AI and art can affect and influence the control and ownership of the art, by creating and generating images, videos, and sounds, that can be uncontrollable and unpredictable, that can deviate and diverge from the user's intention and expectation, and that can confuse and frustrate the user, especially when the user wants to fine-tune or customize the art, and that can affect and influence the authorship and attribution of the art, and that can cause and provoke some legal and ethical questions and issues, such as the originality, authenticity, and creativity of the art, and that can affect and influence the rights and values of the user and others, and that can cause and provoke some negative and adverse reactions and consequences.

- **Ethics**: AI and art can affect and influence the ethics and morality of the art, by creating and generating images, videos, and sounds, that can be unethical and harmful, that can violate and infringe the rights and values of the user and others, and that can cause and provoke some negative and adverse reactions and consequences, especially when the input or output is sensitive, offensive, or illegal, and that can affect and influence the meaning and purpose of the art, and that can challenge and redefine the values and standards of the art.

These and other potential and possibilities, and limitations and challenges, can shape and define the future of AI and art, and what it can and cannot do, and what it can and cannot be. However, the future of AI and art is not fixed or predetermined, it is dynamic and evolving, and it depends on the trends and opportunities, and the implications and impacts, that AI and art can create and face in the next decade and beyond. I will discuss these topics in the next sections.

The emerging and evolving trends and opportunities of AI and art

AI and art have been creating and facing some emerging and evolving trends and opportunities that can shape and define the future of AI and art, and what it can and cannot do, and what it can and cannot be. These trends and opportunities can offer and enable new and different possibilities and options for the user, by using and applying various tools and techniques, such as DALL-E, Discord, Midjourney, and graphic_art, that can create and edit images, videos, and sounds, based on the user's input and feedback.

Some of the emerging and evolving trends and opportunities of AI and art are:

- **Collaboration**: AI and art can offer and enable more and diverse opportunities and resources for collaboration and communication, that can create and share art with a community, that can provide and enable more and diverse feedback, suggestions, and evaluations for art creation and distribution, and that can empower and support the artists and art lovers of different backgrounds, skills, and interests. For example, AI and art can offer and enable collaboration and

58

communication, by using and applying various tools and techniques, such as Discord, that can create and share art with a community, using a chatbot that can generate and modify images, videos, and sounds, based on the user's input and feedback.

- **Interaction**: AI and art can offer and enable more and diverse ways and means of interaction and engagement, that can create and discover art with interaction, that can provide and enable more and diverse ways of input and output, such as text, voice, image, video, and sound, and that can enhance and enrich the artistic expression and experience. For example, AI and art can offer and enable interaction and engagement, by using and applying various tools and techniques, such as graphic_art, that can create art from text, using a neural network that can generate and modify images, based on the text prompt that the user provides.

- **Personalization**: AI and art can offer and enable more and diverse possibilities and options for personalization and customization, that can create and edit art with text, voice, image, video, or sound, that can respond and adjust to the user's input and feedback, and that can accommodate and satisfy the user's preferences and needs, and that can create art that is customized and personalized, based on the user's input and feedback, such as the theme, message, and mood of the art, and the name, logo, and signature of the art. For example, AI and art can offer and enable personalization and customization, by using and applying various tools and techniques, such as Midjourney, that can create and sell art online, using a platform that connects artists and buyers, and that provides various services and features for art creation and distribution.

These and other emerging and evolving trends and opportunities can shape and define the future of AI and art, and what it can and cannot do, and what it can and cannot be. However, the future of AI and art is not only about the trends and opportunities, it is also about the implications and impacts that AI and art can create and face in the next decade and beyond. We will discuss these topics in the next sections.

The ethical and moral implications of AI and art

AI and art have been creating and facing some ethical and moral implications that can shape and define the future of AI and art, and what it means and matters for artists and society. These implications can raise and pose some questions and issues, that can affect and influence the rights and values of the user and others, and that can cause and provoke some negative and adverse reactions and consequences, especially when the input or output is sensitive, offensive, or illegal.

Some of the ethical and moral implications of AI and art are:

- **Originality**: AI and art can raise and pose some questions and issues about the originality and authenticity of the art, such as: Who is the author and owner of the art? Who deserves the credit and recognition for the art? Who has the right and responsibility for the art? How can we define and measure the originality and authenticity of the art? How can we protect and respect the originality and authenticity of the art?
- **Creativity**: AI and art can raise and pose some questions and issues about the creativity and expression of the art, such as: What is the role and contribution of the user and the AI tool in the art? How can we define and measure the creativity and expression of the art? How can we enhance and improve the creativity and expression of the art? How can we balance and harmonize the creativity and expression of the art?
- **Ethics**: AI and art can raise and pose some questions and issues about the ethics and morality of the art, such as: What are the values

and standards of the art? What are the benefits and harms of the art? What are the rights and duties of the user and others in the art? How can we define and apply the ethics and morality of the art? How can we prevent and resolve the ethical and moral conflicts and dilemmas of the art?

These and other ethical and moral implications can shape and define the future of AI and art, and what it means and matters for artists and society. However, the future of AI and art is not only about the implications, it is also about the impacts that AI and art can create and face in the next decade and beyond. We will discuss these topics in the

The social and cultural impacts of AI and art

AI and art have been creating and facing some social and cultural impacts that can shape and define the future of AI and art, and what it means and matters for artists and society. These impacts can affect and influence the perception and appreciation of the art, and the role and contribution of the artists, by creating and changing the social and cultural norms and values, and by creating and challenging the social and cultural issues and conflicts.

Some of the social and cultural impacts of AI and art are:

- **Accessibility**: AI and art can increase and improve the accessibility and availability of the art, by providing and enabling more and diverse opportunities and resources for art creation and distribution, such as the tools, techniques, platforms, and methods, that can lower the barriers and costs of entry and involvement, and that can save and optimize the time and effort of the user, and that can empower and support the artists and art lovers of different backgrounds, skills, and interests, and that can create and enhance the diversity and variety of the art and the audience.

- **Appreciation**: AI and art can affect and influence the appreciation and evaluation of the art, by creating and generating images, videos, and sounds, that can create and change the standards and criteria of the art, such as the originality, authenticity, creativity, quality, and value of the art, and that can affect and influence the perception and recognition of the art, and the credit and reward of the art, and that can create and provoke some questions and issues, such as the authorship, attribution, ownership, and rights of the art, and the ethics, morality, and legality of the art.

- **Expression**: AI and art can affect and influence the expression and communication of the art, by creating and generating images, videos, and sounds, that can create and change the meaning and purpose of the art, such as the thoughts, feelings, and experiences of the user, and the perspective, voice, and message of the user, and that can affect and influence the interaction and engagement of the art, and the impact and change of the art, and that can create and provoke some questions and issues, such as the role and contribution of the user and the AI tool in the art, and the balance and harmony of the user and the AI tool in the art.

These and other social and cultural impacts can shape and define the future of AI and art, and what it means and matters for artists and society. However, the future of AI and art is not only about the impacts, it is also about the preparation and adaptation, that the user and the society can do and make for the future of AI and art, and how to stay ahead of the curve and the game. I will discuss these topics in the next sections.

Review of Chapter 5: The future of AI and art

In this chapter, we have speculated and explored the future of AI and art, and what it means for artists and society. I have discussed topics such as the potential and limitations of AI and art, the emerging and evolving trends and opportunities, the ethical and moral implications, and the social and cultural impacts. I have also given some suggestions and recommendations on how to prepare and adapt for the future of AI and art, and how to stay ahead of the curve and the game.

I hope that this chapter has inspired and challenged you to think and imagine the future of AI and art, and what it can and cannot do, and what it can and cannot be. I also hope that this chapter has shown and taught you the potential and diversity of using AI for art, and how you can use and benefit from the AI tools and techniques effectively and creatively.

This concludes our book on AI Art: The Future of Creativity and How to Profit From It. I hope that you have enjoyed and learned a lot from this book and will use this information to guide you along your own journey in art. I also hope that this book has inspired and will help you to become an inspired and successful AI artist, and that you will contribute added value to the AI art community and society. Thank you for reading this book, and I wish you all the best in your AI and art journey!

7

Conclusion: How to become an AI artist in 2024

AI art is a form of art that uses AI and machine learning to generate and modify images, videos, and sounds, based on the user's input and feedback. AI art can create realistic and diverse art, as well as abstract, surreal, or impossible art, that can inspire and challenge the user's imagination and expression. AI art can also enable and enhance the user's artistic skills and projects, by providing and enabling various tools and techniques, such as DALL-E, Discord, and Midjourney, that can create and edit art for the user.

In this book, I have shown and taught you how to become an AI artist in 2024, by using and applying various tools and techniques, such as DALL-E, Discord, and Midjourney, that can create and edit images, videos, and sounds, based on your input and feedback. I have also shown and taught you how to create amazing AI-generated art, by following and applying a process that consists of five steps: finding inspiration, crafting effective prompts, tweaking and refining the results, adding your own touch and personality, and evaluating and critiquing your own work. I have also shown and taught you how to market and sell your AI-generated art online, and make money in 2024, by defining and applying a business model that consists of five elements: your target market, your pricing strategy, your sales channels, your marketing plan, and your online store. I have also speculated and explored the future of AI and art, and what it means for artists and society, by discussing and analyzing the potential and limitations, the emerging and evolving trends and opportunities, the ethical and moral implications, and the social and cultural impacts of AI and art.

I hope that this book has inspired and helped you to become an AI artist in 2024, and that you will create and share your own amazing AI-generated art, and that this will help you to grow your business from your art. I also hope that this book has shown and taught you the potential and diversity of using AI for art, and how you can use and benefit from the AI tools and techniques effectively and creatively.

I encourage you to take action and apply what you have learned from this book, and to create and share your own AI-generated art, along with growing your business from your art. I also encourage you to keep learning and exploring the AI and art field, and to stay updated and informed about the latest developments and innovations, and to prepare and adapt for the future of AI and art.

I thank you for your time and attention, and we invite you to share your feedback and questions with me. You can join and connect me inside my FaceBook group at this link https://www.facebook.com/grou ps/392564766658073, and I will be happy to hear from you and to help you with your AI and art journey. You can also find some additional learning for further exploration below, and I recommend you to check them out and to expand your knowledge and skills.

Additional learning to check out

AI art is a fascinating and emerging field that combines artificial intelligence and creativity. If you want to learn more about AI art and how to create and sell your own AI artworks, there are some resources that might help you out.

- **How to Create AI Art**: Your Ultimate Guide: A blog post by Skillshare that introduces the concept of AI art and guides you through the steps of creating AI art using different tools and platforms. https://www.skillshare.com/en/blog/how-to—crea te-ai-art-your-ultimate-guide/
- **Free AI Art Course**: An online course by AI Makers Lab that teaches you the basics of AI art, the history and applications of AI art, and the ethical and legal aspects of AI art. You will also learn how to use various AI art tools, such as Midjourney, DALL-E 2, Images AI, and more. https://aimakerslab.io/education/free-ai-art-course/
- **AI Art Generation Guide**: Learn 12+ AI Art Tools: A Udemy course that covers 12+ AI art tools, such as Adobe Firefly, Run-wayML, Leonardo AI, and more. You will learn how to use these tools to create different types of AI art, such as portraits, landscapes, logos, and more. https://www.udemy.com/course/ai-art-generati on-guide/
- **The 20 Best Free AI Art & Image Generation Courses in 2024**: A blog post by Your Dream AI that lists 20 free AI art and image generation courses that you can take in 2024. These courses cover topics such as stability AI, Midjourney, DALL-E 2, and more. https://yourdreamai.com/best-free-ai-art-courses/
- **Artificial Intelligence and Art**: A comprehensive online resource by the MIT Press that explores the intersection of AI and art, featuring articles, case studies, and interviews with AI artists.

https://bing.com/search?q=resources+for+building+AI+Art+journey

These are some additional learning that might help you with your AI art journey. I hope you find them useful and inspiring.

If you found this book helpful, I'd be very appreciative if you left a favorable review for the book on Amazon!

I hope to see you again in my next book, where I will show and teach you how to create and sell your own AI-generated music, and how to profit from it. Stay tuned!

8

Resources

Artificial Intelligence – Mafost blog. (2023, June 8). Mafost Blog. https://mafost.com/tag/artificial-intelligence/

events@homeAI.info. (2018, September 30). The Future of AI at Home: A Conversation between Amazon Alexa and Google Home at AI Frontiers Conference. Events.AI. https://events.ai/2017/11/the-fut ure-of-ai-at-home-a-conversation-between-amazon-alexa-and-googl e-home-at-ai-frontiers-conference/

Joseph. (2022, August 16). Georgia Tech's Machine Learning Professors - reason.town. reason.town. https://reason.town/georgia-tech-machin e-learning-professors/

O'neil, A., & O'neil, A. (2023, June 12). Top SEO and AI terms you must know. #1 Sustainable Link Building and Analytical SEO Agency - 1stpagekws. https://1stpagekws.com/blog/seo-and-ai-terms/

OpenAI. (2024). ChatGPT (January 27 version) [Large language model]. https://chat.openai.com

Sfeir, G. (2011). Critical Media Literacy: A Vehicle For Transformative Learning Towards
   Social And Emotional Competence. https://core.ac.uk/download/21 1511648.pdf

Sharer, H., & Sharer, H. (2023, January 10). What is Music Technology? Exploring the Impact of Digital Revolution on the Music Industry - The Enlightened Mindset. The Enlightened Mindset - Exploring the World of Knowledge and Understanding. https://www.tffn.net/what-is-musi c-technology/

Whitney, L. (2023, December 14). Later, Discord! Midjourney AI tool is moving to dedicated website. ZDNET.
   https://www.zdnet.com/article/later-discord-midjourney-ai-tool-is -moving-to-dedicated-website/

About the Author

Hi, I'm Karla Bonnard, an artist, entrepreneur, and author who is passionate about AI art. I have a degree in Computer Information Systems and a Master's in Education. I taught elementary school for several years before pursuing my dream of becoming a full-time AI artist. I'm also a mom of two amazing teenagers who support me in my artistic endeavors. I love to use AI to create and sell art online, using different tools and techniques, such as DALL-E, Discord, Midjourney, and others. I enjoy creating stunning and unique AI artworks, such as portraits, landscapes, logos, and more. I also enjoy sharing my knowledge and experience with other aspiring AI artists and helping them learn and profit from the AI art revolution. That's why I wrote my book, AI Art: The Future of Creativity and How to Profit from It. It's a comprehensive and practical guide on how to use AI to create and sell art online in 2024 and how to prepare for the future of AI and art. I hope my book will inspire and empower you to unleash your creativity and help you profit from AI art.

You can connect with me on:

🅵 https://www.facebook.com/groups/392564766658073

Made in the USA
Monee, IL
29 March 2024